this book is presented to

_____

by

_____

date

_____

_____

_____

This poem is dedicated to Savannah Joy
my beautiful granddaughter. My prayer is that you find the true meaning of
Christmas – Jesus living in your heart – at an early age.

Love,

Papa
12/99

ISBN - 9780615226897
Text Copyright 2008 by Timothy Penland
Illustrations Copyright 2008 by Savannah Joy Adams
All Rights Reserved

canecreekpublishers

162 Wilson Road
Fairview, NC 28730
www.canecreekpublishers.com

text is presented in Skia -20

Printed in Reynosa, Tamaulipas Mexico
December 2010
4 5 6 7 8 9 10 11/15 14 13 12 11 10

the True Night before Christmas

Timothy Penland

illustrated by Savannah Joy Adams

'Twas the night before Christmas
But it's not what you thought,

This is not about Santa
Or presents you've bought.

It's about the Christ Child
Who was born as a boy,
Who brought the world Peace
And gave my heart Joy.

To Bethlehem of Judea
Mary and Joseph were sent,
To record there – their names
For Rome's government.

When they got there, they found
They had no place to stay,
And Mary felt sure
Christ would come any day.

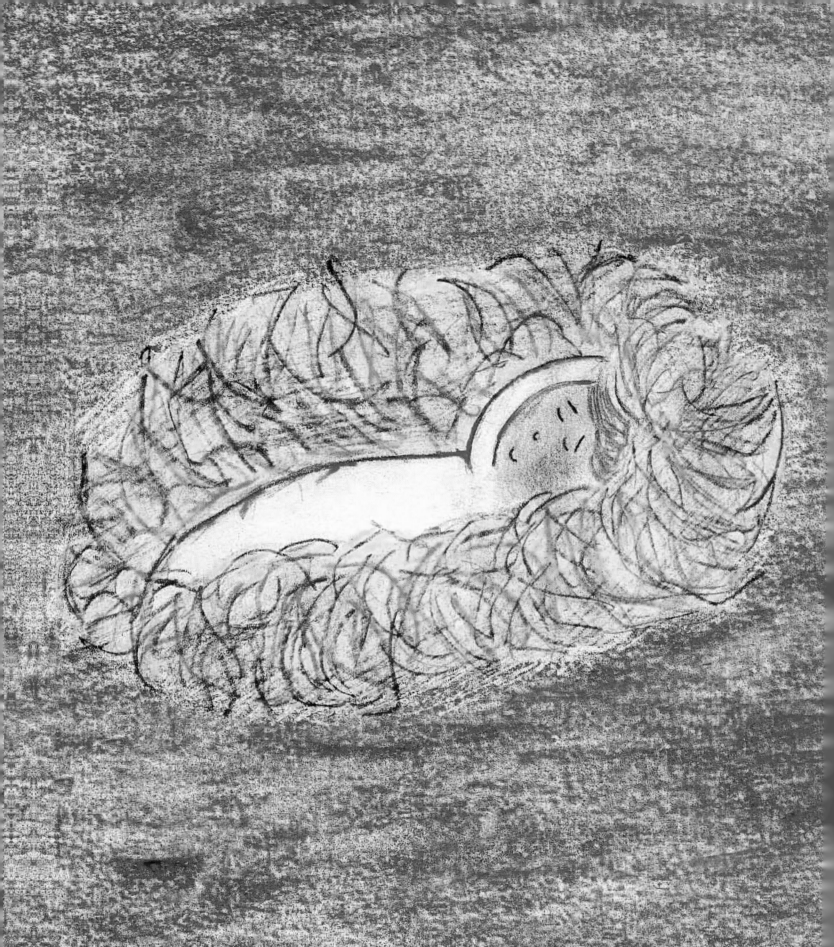

Then they came to a stable,
A place they could stay
And Jesus was born
Right there in the hay.

Mary wrapped Him in cloths
That very first night,
Then He slept in a manger
Jesus – God's light.

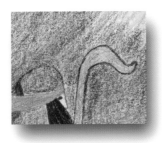

Not too far from there
Shepherds tended their sheep.
Then an angel appeared
And no one could sleep.

"Don't be afraid"
The angel cried out,
"I have some good news
You'll like it – NO DOUBT!"

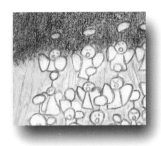

A whole choir of angels
All started singing,
With that many voices
The hills were all ringing.

The men headed to town
To see this new child,
They found him right there
So meek and so mild.

They left praising God
For what they had seen,
And told everyone
Where the Christ-child had been.

There were also three Wisemen
Who wanted to see
This new child from heaven-
Come to save you and me.

They had seen a great star
In the dark eastern night,
And rode on their camels
Being led by its light.

They came to a city
And met with the king,
They thought he would help them
And end their searching.

He was evil and bad
And no friend of what's good,
He would help them find Jesus-
To kill if he could.

The king called all the priests
They'd know where He'd be,
"In Judea" they said,
"Now go there and see."

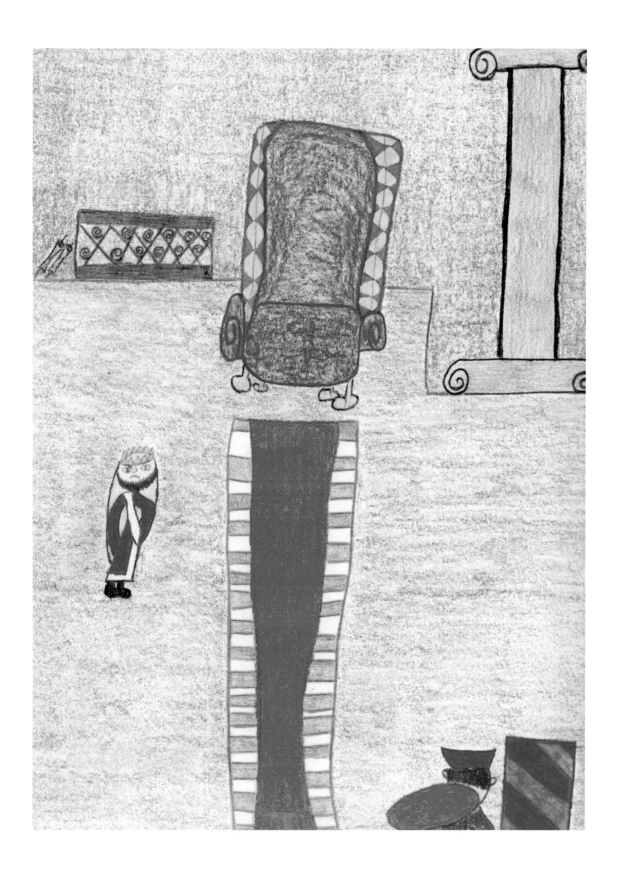

So the Wisemen left town
And the star went before,
'Til it stopped once again
At Jesus' front door.

The Wisemen went in-
Gave Jesus their presents.
They brought with them gold,
Myrrh and precious incense.

They went home a new way
'Cause an angel had said,
"The king will kill Jesus,
Now go where I've led."

So Mary and Joseph
Had all these great guests,
Who came to see Jesus
On whom God's favor rests.

For He was God's gift
To bring us salvation,
To cleanse us from sin
And take us to heaven.

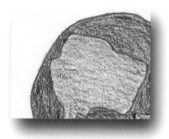

This is not just a kid's tale
The facts are all true.
Jesus lived on this earth
And He died just for you.

Yes, He came for us all
Not just in a manger,
But to die on a cross
And save us from danger.

Jesus one day would die
On that old rugged cross,
And save us from sin
So we would not be lost.

He'll come to our hearts
And make us God's children.
He'll always be with us
And take us to heaven.

All those who believe Him
Who trust in His light,

Know He brought the true Christmas.
Now to all a good night.

Acknowledgments

Thanks to so many who have provided the help and encouragement that brought this book into reality. Special thanks to Joy, my wife of over 30 years for her support and unfailing confidence. Her unique perspective comes from many years in a Kindergarten classroom.

Thank you seems insufficient to express the importance of family in my life, and in the completion of this project. Angie, Ben, and later Brett gave me the opportunity to display my love of the Christmas season. Their gifts were instrumental in making this project come to life. Savannah, Elizabeth, and Emma listened to my stories and poems. Mom and Dad demonstrated a love for the Lord Jesus in their daily lives, and shared that love with all of their offspring.

Savannah's artwork makes the story come alive, in part because of her artistic talent. More importantly, it displays her understanding of the true Reason we have the Season.

Angie's guidance and support for Savannah's work was immeasurably important to the completion of the process.

Thanks to Dot for her encouragement and support, and to Kirk for his continuing help with the publishing and editing. Special thanks to Mike Miller and all of our friends at Navpress (especially Jessica Chappell) for their friendship, counsel, guidance, and help in advancing this dream.

Most of all, thank you to our Lord Jesus Christ. He was willing to come to this earth over 2000 years ago. His life, death, and resurrection is the only reason there was a Night Before Christmas.

Timothy Penland

The text of this book is based upon the following scripture passages:

Luke 2: 1-20
Matthew 2: 1-12
Luke 1: 26-28, 35
John 3:16
Romans 6: 23
John 1: 1-5
Luke 19: 10